D1014801

The publisher would like to thank the following for
their kind permission to reproduce their photographs:
(Abbreviations key : t=top, b=bottom, r=right, l=left, c=centre,
tl=top left, tr=top right, bl=bottom left, br=bottom right)

Cover: Tim Graham Picture Library/Corbis
2: Hulton Deutsch Collection/Corbis; 3: Corbis; 4: Camera Press/James Veysey; 5: Rex Features;
6: Topfoto (t), Hip/ARPL/Topfoto (b); 7: Topfoto; 8: Rex Features; 9: Topfoto (t), Topfoto/PA (b);
10: Topfoto (t), Topfoto/PA (b); 11: Topfoto; 12: Topfoto (t), Rex Features (c), Topfoto (b);
13: Topfoto; 14: Bettmann/Corbis (t), Topfoto (b); 15: Bettmann/Corbis; 16: Rex Features (t),
Sipa/Rex Features (b); 17: Topfoto/PA (t), Times Newspapers/Rex Features (b); 18: AC
Searle/Rex Features (t), Rex Features (b); 19: Topfoto/PA (tl), Mauro Carraro/Rex Features (tr),
Topfoto (b); 20: David Wootton/Alamy (t), Tim Graham/Corbis (b); 21: David Gowans/Alamy (t),
Alex Segre/Rex Features (b); 22: Topfoto (t), Norman Parkinson/Fiona Cowan/Corbis (bl), Tim
Graham Picture Library/Corbis (br); 23: Rex Features (t), Pool/Tim Graham Picture
Library/Corbis (b); 24: Joan Williams/Rex Features; 25: AFP/Getty Images; 26: Peter
Brooker/Rex Features; 27: David Levenson/Rex Features (t), Peter Brooker/Rex Features (b);
28: Michael Dunlea/Rex Features (t), Camera Press/London (b); 29: Camera Press/Julian Calder;
30: Rex Features 31: Camera Press/London

Published by Ladybird Books Ltd
80 Strand, London, WC2R ORL
A Penguin Company
2 4 6 8 10 9 7 5 3 1
© Ladybird Books Ltd 2006

Printed in Italy

HER MAJESTY
THE QUEEN

When Elizabeth was born, no one thought that she would be Queen. On the day her grandfather King George V died, her uncle succeeded him to the throne as Edward VIII.

Elizabeth in her pram

Unfortunately Edward wanted to marry a divorced lady, and in those days a king was not allowed to do that. So Edward gave up the throne to marry, and Elizabeth's father became King George VI in his place.

Elizabeth as a child on the steps of Y Bwthn Bach, the playhouse given to her by the people of Wales

Elizabeth knew then that she would probably be Queen – unless a little brother came along. She used to pray for that to happen!

Although now very much in the public eye, the King and Queen tried hard to give their two daughters a proper family life. Elizabeth and her sister Margaret Rose enjoyed a happy childhood.

Elizabeth and her sister Margaret

As a teenager, Princess Elizabeth was very pretty, with sparkling blue eyes and lovely skin.

She met her future husband Prince Philip of Greece in 1939, not long before the start of World War II. He was eighteen at the time, and just off to war as a sailor. He was a brave young man, and was held in high regard in the navy.

Elizabeth did her bit during the war, just like other girls of her age. Here she is changing a tyre

Elizabeth with her fiancé Lieutenant Philip Mountbatten at a ball in Edinburgh, Scotland, 16th July 1947

All through the war, Philip wrote to his princess, and went to see her when he was on leave. Although King George liked him, they had to wait to marry until things settled down at the end of the war.

Elizabeth and Lieut. Philip Mountbatten pose for their first engagement photos

The country was just beginning to recover from the effects of a long war. This, the first Royal wedding for many years, was welcomed with joy.

Everything was still rationed, even clothes. Nylon stockings, for example, were in very short supply, but girls from all over Britain sent pairs to Elizabeth as a present.

The wedding cake

The happy couple on the balcony of Buckingham Palace

Everyone was pleased that she was marrying such a handsome young man. Philip was a real heartthrob, with a lovely smile. He also had a sense of fun and was very good company.

Elizabeth had chosen her partner for life well.

Elizabeth on her wedding day

Britain rejoiced in 1948 at the birth of Elizabeth's first son, Charles, the new heir to the throne. Shops closed everywhere and the armed forces were given time off to celebrate.

Then in 1950 Princess Anne was born. Elizabeth had been Queen for eight years when her second son, Andrew, was born, to be followed four years later by Edward.

The Queen and Philip (now Duke of Edinburgh) broke with tradition by being the first royals to send their children to school.

The boys went to Philip's old school in Scotland – Gordonstoun – and daughter Anne went to Benenden, a girls' school in Kent.

A Gordonstoun dormitory in 1962

In 1952 came the moment Elizabeth had always dreaded – her father died and she became Queen. Her coronation in 1953 was an international and magnificent spectacle. Elizabeth took her vows with great dignity, recognising the awesome responsibility that had fallen on her. She would never let her subjects down.

Another great event signalled well for the new reign. A Commonwealth team conquered Everest – the highest mountain in the world – that very same day.

Sir Edmund Hillary of the British Everest Expedition, 2 June 1953

Queen Elizabeth's official coronation portrait

Now that Elizabeth was Head of State, she had many new duties to perform. There were documents to read and sign, consultations with the Prime Minister, many people to meet, and she had to take part in lots of ceremonies.

She also became Britain's greatest ambassador abroad, ably supported by Prince Philip. She has always been elegantly dressed for every occasion, and well prepared with the right things to say at any function.

The Queen with Mother Theresa, August 1985

The Queen follows etiquette rigidly, never putting a foot wrong. However, at one grand dinner, she took out her powder compact. She powdered her nose, put the compact back in her bag, then rose to make her speech. The rules were changing . . .

Even the Queen's horses know their manners, and stand completely still. The photo above was taken by John Scott, the Queen's favourite photographer. She was always slightly self-conscious about her nose, and used to ask him wistfully if he could make it look smaller

The Queen enjoying a joke during a tour of Africa

In common with most British people, the Royal Family has always loved animals. Horses were Elizabeth's first love, followed by her dogs and the blue budgies she was fond of.

The Queen's favourite dogs have always been Welsh Corgis, but now her dogs also include Dorgis – a cross between a Dachshund and a Corgi.

Elizabeth has loved dogs all her life

The Queen's dogs are cheerful and affectionate, and as these pictures show, they love their mistress. The Queen is rarely to be seen without them when relaxing at home.

Buckingham Palace is the Queen's main home, but she has many others. She adores Scotland and her home there is called Balmoral. The Royal Family goes there to relax, as they also do at Sandringham in Norfolk.

Sandringham from the air

The Queen also has a home called Windsor Castle. Once a fire destroyed many valuable objects inside. Fortunately, the castle was soon restored, and people queued to see the results.

Balmoral Castle

You would think a Queen would be safe in her own palace, where there are sentries at the gates and people to guard her. But once, a man managed to get into her bedroom. It turned out he only wanted to talk to her, but it must have been a frightening experience for a lady in her own home.

Mothers take pride in their families, and the Queen is no exception. She was delighted when daughter Anne took part in the Olympics.

Mothers also worry about their families. Prince Andrew fought in the Falklands War as a naval helicopter pilot and was often in dangerous situations. Waiting and wondering if your son will return safely is a heavy burden for any mother to bear.

When children grow up and marry, they can have domestic problems. Parents do their best to help, but sometimes nothing can make it better. People get divorced and find new partners.

HRH Princess Anne with her first husband Captain Mark Phillips on their Wedding Day, 1973, and with her second husband, Commodore Timothy Laurence at a Service of Remembrance for the Iraq War, 2003

Charles and Diana's wedding, 1981

Prince Charles with his new bride and second wife Camilla, Duchess of Cornwall, with Prince Harry far left and Prince William next on the left

Work is as much an everyday matter for the Queen as for any of her subjects. For all public engagements, wherever they take place, she must be fully prepared.

Her Majesty the Queen, December 1985

She also has plenty of paperwork connected with the Royal estates and the charities she supports to keep her busy.

Her Majesty also has to read state papers every day, and has a weekly consultation with the Prime Minister.

It's a busy life and can be very tiring for a lady of eighty!

Tony Blair arriving at Buckingham Palace, May 2005

One of the great pleasures in life for the Queen is horse racing. She owns and races many horses, and loves it when they win.

The Queen Mother, the Queen and Princess Anne on Derby Day, 1988

The Royal Meeting takes place each year over four days during June at Ascot, the Queen's own racecourse. At the start of racing each day, the Queen and the royal party are driven round the course in carriages to greet the racegoers.

Princess Michael, wife to Prince Michael of Kent, is also a keen racegoer

Ladies Day at Ascot is a day to remember, with the champagne flowing. The gentlemen wear top hats and morning suits, and the ladies wear fancy hats, whether they are royal or not!

A rare display of emotion as the Queen's horse crosses the finishing line

As life goes on, sad things happen. Loved ones die, such as Diana, Princess of Wales, mother to Princes William and Harry.

In 2002, the Queen Mother died. As well as the Queen's much-loved Mum, she was also Queen Mum to millions. Sadly also in 2002, the Queen's sister Princess Margaret died.

So to the lady who has just turned eighty, who's always done her Royal duty and kept faith with her people, we say…

Three generations of the Royal Family pose at Clarence House, London

Happy Birthday,
Your Majesty!

21st April 1926
Princess Elizabeth's birth

2nd June 1953
Elizabeth's Coronation as
Queen Elizabeth II

21st August 1930
Princess Margaret's birth

6th February 1952
Death of Elizabeth's father,
King George VI

15th August 1950
Princess Anne's birth

14th November 1948
Prince Charles's birth

20th November 1947
Elizabeth's wedding
to Prince Philip of Greece

12th May 1937
Coronation of
Elizabeth's father,
King George VI

20th January 1936
Death of Elizabeth's
grandfather,
King George V

10th December 1936
Abdication of
Elizabeth's uncle,
Edward VIII